Puffin Books

THE PUFFIN MONSTE

At last you are able to lay you
collection of the world's wors
idiots' guide to loathsome creatures you can terrify your
teacher, petrify your parents and amuse your friends.
From witches and vampires to werewolves and skeletons
– all the jokes in this book are truly monstrous.

Warning – you may find yourself struck down with a
bad attack of the giggles. We recommend you turn to the
special introduction before proceeding.

Martyn Forrester, journalist and monster enthusiast,
has spent many years getting to know the world's most
loathsome creatures and collecting their jokes. David
McKee has brought to this collection his unique talent for
making you giggle at the grotesque.

For Iona

MARTYN FORRESTER

THE PUFFIN
MONSTER
JOKE BOOK

Illustrated by David McKee

PUFFIN BOOKS

PUFFIN BOOKS

Penguin Books Ltd, Harmondsworth, Middlesex, England
Viking Penguin Inc., 40 West 23rd Street, New York, New York 10010, USA
Penguin Books Australia Ltd, Ringwood, Victoria, Australia
Penguin Books Canada Ltd, 2801 John Street, Markham, Ontario,
Canada L3R 1B4
Penguin Books (N.Z.) Ltd, 182–190 Wairau Road, Auckland 10, New Zealand

First published 1987

Copyright © Martyn Forrester, 1987
Illustrations copyright © David McKee, 1987
All rights reserved

Set in Linotron Palatino by
Rowland Phototypesetting Ltd
Bury St Edmunds, Suffolk
Made and printed in Great Britain by
Cox & Wyman Ltd, Reading, Berks

Dear Human,

Do you know when monsters play jokes on each other? April Ghoul's Day.

And do you know where they get all their jokes from? The Puffin Monster Joke Book, of course!

Yes be warned, human – you are now entering the scariest, creepiest, slimiest, ugliest, most *monstrous* joke book ever written. If you're at all the nervous type, put it down now and walk quietly away. This is NOT a book for non-monsters . . .

I know the author well. When we first met I took him home for dinner – I thought he'd be delicious with a few pickled bunions, fish fungus and a bit of eyes-cream. But I found him too hard to swallow. 'Just goes to show,' he said, 'you can't keep a good man down.'

Then he took me on a world cruise. As we took our seats in the dining room, the waiter came up and asked if we'd like to see the menu. 'No thank you,' I replied politely. 'Just bring me the passenger list . . .'

I was a bit worried when he asked me to write this introduction. I'd never written anything before. In the end I had to rush out and eat a few joke writers, just to get the flavour of it.

So here we are, The Introduction:

BOO!

Well, must be off now. It's the Skeletons' Fete this afternoon, and I'm in charge of the rattle tickets . . .

With best vicious
Yours gruesomely,

Your Editor

Did you hear about the witch who lost her bus fare?
She had to witch-hike home.

What phantom was a famous painter?
Vincent Van Ghost.

How do you stop a monster from smelling?
Cut off his nose.

What do you do with a green monster?
Wait until it ripens!

Why didn't the skeleton want to go to school?
Because his heart wasn't in it.

What do they have for lunch at Monster School?
Human beans, boiled legs, pickled bunions and eyes-cream.

Which monster eats the fastest?
The goblin.

What do you call a TV show that stars ghosts and phantoms?
A spook-tacular.

What's a skeleton?
Bones, with the people scraped off.

FIRST GHOST: My bike is always breaking down. I think it must be jinxed.
SECOND GHOST: *Maybe you've got a spook in your wheel.*

What do you call a monster with a sausage on its head?
A head-banger.

What do you call ghost children?
Boys and Ghouls.

Which skeleton was once Emperor of France?
Napoleon Bone-apart.

What does a polite vampire say?
'Fang you very much.'

Did you hear what happened to Frankenstein's monster?
He was stopped for speeding, fined £150 and dismantled for six months.

What is a vampire's favourite fruit?
Blood oranges.

What is a vampire's second favourite fruit?
Neck-tarines.

How does a vampire get through life with only one fang?
He has to grin and bare it.

Where does a vampire take a bath?
In a bat tub.

What do you call a monster with a spade in his head?
Doug.

What's a vampire's favourite dance?
The vaults.

What's a vampire's second favourite dance?
The fang-dango.

What's pink, has a curly tail, and drinks blood?
A hampire.

Why are vampires sometimes called simple-minded?
Because they're known to be suckers.

Where does a vampire save his money?
At the blood bank.

FIRST MONSTER: I had a nice man to dinner last night.
SECOND MONSTER: So you enjoyed having him?
FIRST MONSTER: *Oh yes . . . he was delicious.*

What did the vampire say to his girlfriend?
'After the film, do you fancy a bite?'

How do ghosts begin a letter?
'Tomb it may concern . . .'

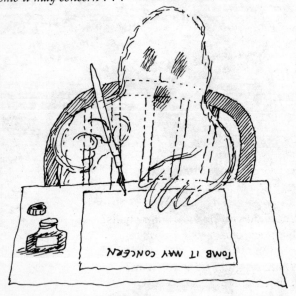

How do witches drink tea?
With cups and sorcerers.

What did one invisible man say to the other?
'It's nice not to see you again.'

'Doctor, doctor, I keep feeling like the invisible man.'
'Who said that?'

What do you call a witch who goes to the beach but won't go into the water?
A chicken sand-witch.

What kind of plate does a skeleton eat off?
Bone china.

Who appears on the cover of horror magazines?
The cover ghoul!

What is Dracula's favourite breakfast?
Readyneck.

Was Dracula ever married?
No, he was a bat-chelor.

Where do you find monster snails?
On the end of monsters fingers.

Where do ghosts like to swim?
In the Dead Sea.

What did the policeman say when he met the three-headed monster?
''Allo, 'allo, 'allo.'

What is the monsters' favourite football team?
Slitherpool.

What is the ghosts' favourite Wild West town?
Tombstone.

Why wouldn't the skeleton jump off the cliff?
Because he had no guts.

What's a monster's favourite fairground ride?
The Roller Ghoster.

What is Dracula's favourite pudding?
Leeches and scream.

Where do ghosts study?
At ghoul-lege.

What is the ghosts' favourite pub?
The Horse and Gloom.

What is a monster's favourite drink?
Demonade.

Why are monsters' fingers never more than eleven inches long?
Because if they were twelve inches they'd be a foot.

What is the best thing to do if a monster breaks down your front door?
Run out of the back door.

IGOR: Why is Baron Frankenstein such good fun?
MONSTER: *Because he soon has you in stitches.*

Did you hear about Romeo Monster meeting Juliet Monster?
It was love at first fright.

Why was Baron Frankenstein never lonely?
Because he was good at making friends.

Why did the skeleton go to the party?
To have a rattling good time!

Why do monsters have trouble swallowing priests and vicars?
Because it's hard to keep a good man down.

Why did the baby monster push his father into the freezer?
Because he wanted frozen pop.

What is a ghost's favourite music?
Haunting melodies.

Why does Dracula live in a coffin?
Because the rent is low.

What do you call twin ghosts who keep ringing door-bells?
Dead ringers.

What game do ghosts like to play at parties?
Haunt and seek.

What does an Indian ghost live in?
A creepy teepee.

Who puts the ghosts' point of view at their press conference?
A spooksman.

Can a toothless vampire still bite you?
No, but he can give you a nasty suck!

Who brings the monsters their babies?
Frankenstork.

Who said 'Shiver me timbers!' on the ghost ship?
The skeleton crew.

What job did the lady ghost have on the jumbo jet?
Air ghostess.

Why are monsters so forgetful?
Because everything you tell them goes in one ear and out the others.

Did you hear about the stupid ghost?
He climbed over walls.

Why did Frankenstein's monster give up boxing?
Because he didn't want to spoil his looks.

What do monsters put on their roast beef?
Grave-y.

What is the best way to speak to a monster?
From a long distance.

The ghost teacher was showing her class how to walk through walls. 'Now did you all understand that?' she asked. 'If not, I'll just go through it again . . .'

Where do space monsters live?
In far distant terror-tory.

Which is the ghosts' favourite stretch of water?
Lake Eerie.

What do you do if you see a skeleton running across the road?
Jump out of your skin and join him.

What is it called when a vampire gets a lot of letters from his admirers?
Fang mail.

Why did the mummy leave his tomb after 4,000 years?
He felt he was old enough to leave home.

What did the estate agent say to the ghost?
'I'm sorry, sir, we have nothing suitable for haunting at the moment.'

What did the ghost sentry say?
'Who ghosts there?'

What do baby ghosts like chewing?
Booble gum.

What's it called when a vampire kisses you good night?
Necking.

What trees do monsters like best?
Ceme-trees.

FATHER MONSTER: Johnny, don't make faces at that man. I've told you before, you mustn't play with your food.

What is the best way for a ghost hunter to keep fit?
Exorcise regularly.

What is Dracula's favourite sport?
Bat-minton.

FIRST MONSTER: Am I late for dinner?
SECOND MONSTER: *Yes, everyone's been eaten.*

What does a vampire take for a bad cold?
Coffin drops.

Did you hear about the girl monster who wasn't pretty and wasn't ugly?
She was pretty ugly.

What is bright red and dumb?
A blood clot.

Why do demons and ghouls get on so well?
Because demons are a ghoul's best friend.

What kind of music do witches play on the piano?
Hag-time.

Which monster made friends with three bears?
Ghouldilocks.

'I used to be a werewolf, but I'm all right
nowoooooooooooo!'

Count Dracula has denied that he is to marry Princess
Vampire.
They're just going to remain good fiends.

What did Frankenstein's monster say when he was
struck by lightning?
'Great! That was just what I needed.'

MONSTER WIFE: I don't know what to make of my
husband.
FRIEND: *How about a hotpot?*

Why did the vampire actress turn down so many film
offers?
She was waiting for a part that she could get her teeth into.

What is twenty metres long, ugly, and sings 'Scotland The Brave'?
The Loch Ness Songster.

What's big, green and smells?
A monster's bottom.

What did the skeleton say to his girlfriend?
'I love every bone in your body.'

Why are ghosts simple things?
Because you can see right through them.

What do monsters do every night at 11 o'clock?
Take a coffin break.

What jewels do monsters wear?
Tomb stones.

Who has feathers and fangs and goes 'quack, quack'?
Count Duckula.

Why did the Cyclops give up teaching?
He only had one pupil.

Which is the monster's favourite ballet?
Swamp Lake.

Why did the two Cyclops fight?
They could never see eye-to-eye over anything.

FIRST GIRL: Yesterday I took my boyfriend to see *The Monster From The Swamp* at the cinema.
SECOND GIRL: *What was he like?*
FIRST GIRL: Oh, about ten feet tall, with a horrible, slimy head, and a bolt through his neck.
SECOND GIRL: *I don't mean your boyfriend, silly – what was the monster like?*

What goes out only at night and goes 'Chomp, suck . . . ouch!'?
A vampire with a rotten fang.

How can you tell a monster from an elephant?
A monster never remembers.

What did the monster eat after its teeth were pulled out?
The dentist.

How did Frankenstein's monster eat its food?
By bolting it down.

What's the difference between a monster and a mouse?
A monster makes bigger holes in the skirting board.

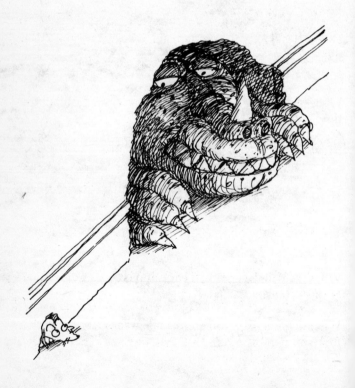

Where do the cleanest monsters live?
Bath.

What do you call a female monster with a piano on her head?
Joanna.

What do you call a monster who gets up your nose?
Vic.

Did you hear about the monster who went on a crash diet?
He wrecked three cars and a bus.

What do you call a monster who lies on the floor all the time?
Matt.

Did you hear about the monster who ate a sofa and two chairs?
He had a suite tooth.

What do you call a monster who's black and blue all over?
Bruce.

What is small, has pointed ears, and is a great detective?
Sherlock Gnomes.

What do you get if you cross a tall green monster with a fountain pen?
The Ink-credible Hulk.

Did you hear about the monster with five legs?
His trousers fit him like a glove.

What do you get if you cross a monster's brain with an elastic band?
A real stretch of the imagination.

Where is the Martian's temple?
On the side of his head.

What do you call a monster lying in the gutter?
Dwayne.

What do you call a monster who sits on a pile of wood?
Guy.

A gang of vampires broke into a blood-bank last night and stole a thousand pints of blood.
Police are still hunting for the clots.

What do you call a female monster who climbs up walls?
Ivy.

What's the difference between a witch and the letters M,A,K,E,S?
One makes spells and the other spells makes.

What do you call a monster with an entire police station on his head?
Nick.

What do you call a monster with an oil rig on his head?
Derek.

Never Make a Girl Monster Angry by Sheila Tack.

What should you do if you find yourself in the same room as Frankenstein, Dracula, a werewolf, a vampire and a coven of witches?
Keep your fingers crossed that it's a fancy dress party.

FIRST MONSTER: That girl over there just rolled her eyes at me.
SECOND MONSTER: *Well, roll them back, she might need them.*

Three monsters called Manners, Mind-Your-Own-Business and Trouble were on a day's outing from the circus, when all of a sudden Trouble went missing. Being good friends of his, Manners and Mind-Your-Own-Business decided to report Trouble missing.

When they got to the police station, Manners got frightened and decided to stay outside. Mind-You-Own-Business went in to report the loss. The desk sergeant asked him his name, to which the monster replied, 'Mind-Your-Own-Business.'

The desk sergeant crossly said, 'Where's your manners?'

Mind-Your-Own-Business replied, 'Outside.'

On hearing such rudeness, the desk sergeant said, 'Are you looking for Trouble?' to which Mind-Your-Own-Business quickly replied, 'Yes, please!'

A woman with a baby in her arms was sitting in a station waiting room, sobbing miserably. A porter came up to her and asked what the trouble was.

'Some people were in here just now and they were so rude about my little boy,' she cried. 'They all said he was horribly ugly.'

'There, there, don't cry,' said the porter kindly. 'Shall I get you a nice cup of tea?'

'Thank you, that would be nice,' replied the woman, wiping her eyes. 'You're very kind.'

'That's all right. Don't mention it,' said the porter. 'While I'm at it, by the way, would you like a banana for your little gorilla?'

What's a monster's favourite soup?
Scream of tomato.

What is Dracula's favourite song?
Fangs For The Memory . . .

What do you call a gorilla who works as a car mechanic?
A grease monkey.

What do you call a gorilla with two bananas in his ears?
Anything you like, because he can't hear you.

GORILLA: Doctor, my hair keeps falling out. What can you give me to keep it in?
DOCTOR: *Try this cardboard box.*

GORILLA: Doctor, I don't know what's the matter with me. I've gone right off bananas and spend all day dreaming about apples.
DOCTOR: *Cor!*

Knock, knock.
Who's there?
Gorilla.
Gorilla who?
Gorilla cheese sandwich for me and I'll be right over.

A gorilla was walking through the jungle when he came across a deer eating grass in a clearing. The gorilla roared, 'Who is the king of the jungle?' and the deer replied, 'Oh, you are, Master.'

The gorilla walked off pleased. Soon he came across a zebra drinking at a water hole. The gorilla roared, 'Who is the king of the jungle?' and the zebra replied, 'Oh, you are, Master.'

The gorilla walked off pleased. Then he came across an elephant. 'Who is the king of the jungle?' he roared. With that, the elephant threw the gorilla across a tree and jumped on him. The gorilla scraped himself up off the ground and said, 'Okay, okay, there's no need to get mad just because you don't know the answer.'

FRED: Did I ever tell you about the time I came face to face with a very fierce gorilla?

BERT: No, what happened?
FRED: Well, I stood there, without a gun . . . The gorilla looked at me and snarled and roared and beat his chest. Then it came closer and closer . . .
BERT: What did you do?
FRED: Oh, I'd had enough, so I moved on to the next cage.

What do you do if you find a gorilla in your bed?
Sleep somewhere else.

What do you do if you want toast in the jungle?
Put it under the g'riller.

What did the grape say when the gorilla stood on it?
Nothing – it just gave a little wine.

A man thought he had swallowed a monster, and nothing his doctor said would make him change his mind. So, finally the doctor gave him an anaesthetic and put him into a deep sleep. When he woke up, the doctor was standing beside his bed, holding a great big green monster on a lead.

   'Nothing more to worry about,' he said. 'We operated on you and took him out.'

   'Who are you trying to kid?' said the man. 'The one I swallowed was a blue one.'

A policeman stopped a man who was walking along with a monster and ordered him to take it to the zoo at once. The next day the policeman saw the same man, still with the monster.

'I thought I told you to take that monster to the zoo,' he said.

'I did,' said the man, 'and now I'm taking him to the pictures.'

What's big and ugly and goes up and down?
A monster in a lift.

What's big and ugly and drinks out of the wrong side of the glass?
A monster trying to get rid of hiccups.

What's big and ugly and takes aspirins?
A monster with a headache.

What do you call a monster that's small and attractive?
A failure.

Why did the monster dye her hair yellow?
To see if blondes have more fun.

What's big and ugly and wears sunglasses?
A monster on holiday.

What's big and ugly and bounces?
A monster on a pogo stick.

What's big and ugly and found at twenty fathoms?
A monster with an aqualung.

What's big and ugly with red spots?
A monster with measles.

What's big and ugly and has eight wheels?
A monster on roller skates.

What's big and ugly and goes at 125 m.p.h.?
A monster on an Inter-City train.

Why did the Invisible Man look in the mirror?
To make sure he still wasn't there!

What do you call it when a ghost makes a mistake?
A boo-boo.

What is a monster's favourite TV programme?
Horror-nation Street.

Where do monsters go on holiday?
From ghost to ghost.

FRIEND TO MONSTER MOTHER: Goodness, hasn't your little girl grown!
MONSTER MOTHER: *Yes, she's certainly gruesome!*

What is a ghost's favourite day of the week?
Moanday.

FIRST HUMAN BOY: Why do you keep throwing bunches of garlic out of the window?
SECOND HUMAN BOY: *To keep the vampires away.*
FIRST HUMAN BOY: But there are no vampires around here.
SECOND HUMAN BOY: *Jolly effective, isn't it?*

What runs around Paris at lunchtime in a plastic bag?
The lunch-pack of Notre Dame.

MRS MONSTER: Will you love me when I'm old and ugly?
MR MONSTER: *Darling, of course I do.*

BOY MONSTER: What would you like for your birthday, sis?
GIRL MONSTER: *I'd love a frock to match the colour of my eyes.*
BOY MONSTER: All right, but where am I going to get a bloodshot dress?

'Here's a good book,' said the sales assistant in the book shop to Mrs Monster. *'How To Help Your Husband Get Ahead.'* 'No, thank you,' said Mrs Monster. 'My husband's got two heads already . . .'

A man went into a pub with a big, vicious looking monster on a lead. 'Sorry, sir,' said the barman, 'but that creature looks dangerous. You'll have to tie him up outside.'

So the man took the monster outside, and came back and ordered a drink. He was just finishing it when a lady came into the bar and said, 'Whose monster is that outside?'

'Mine,' said the man, beaming with pride.

'Well, I'm sorry,' the lady said, 'but my dog's just killed him.'

'Killed him! What kind of dog do you have?'

'A miniature poodle,' said the lady.

'But how could a miniature poodle kill my great big monster?'

'She got stuck in his throat and choked him . . .'

A very tall monster with several arms and legs, all of different lengths, went into a tailor's shop.

'I'd like to see a suit that will fit me,' he told the tailor.

'So would I, sir,' said the tailor. 'So would I.'

What do ghosts call their navy?
The Ghost Guard.

How do ghosts pass through a locked door?
With a skeleton key.

What do you get if you cross a midget with Dracula?
A vampire that sucks blood from your kneecaps.

How does a worried ghost look?
Grave.

Why are vampires crazy?
Because they are often bats.

What do you flatten a ghost with?
A spirit-level.

What did the barman say when the ghost ordered a gin and tonic?
'Sorry, we don't serve spirits.'

How does a witch tell the time?
She wears a witch-watch.

Where does Dracula get all his jokes?
From his crypt-writer.

What do you get if you cross a yeti with a kangaroo?
A fur coat with big pockets.

Two monsters fell off a cliff – boom boom!

What's the quickest way to escape from a monster?
Run!

What is a monster who is married with seven children called?
Daddy.

What do you give a seasick monster?
Plenty of room!

When is a bogey-man most likely to enter your bedroom?
When the door is open.

Why would nobody visit the posh ghost?
Because he had such a ghastly manor.

MONSTER BOY: Should you eat chicken with your fingers?
MONSTER MUM: *No, fingers should be eaten separately.*

What do you get if you cross Dracula with a hot dog?
A fangfurter.

PATIENT: Doctor, can a person be in love with a monster?
DOCTOR: *No.*
PATIENT: Oh. Do you know anyone who wants to buy an extremely large engagement ring then . . .?

Where do ghosts go to church?
Westmonster Abbey.

When do ghosts haunt skyscrapers?
When they are in high spirits.

If storks bring human babies, what bring monster babies?
Cranes.

A headless ghost went to the Lost Property Department.
The man behind the desk looked up, and said: 'Sorry,
mate, I can't help you. You need our Head Office . . .'

Did you hear about the two-headed monster at the freak
show who went on strike for more money?
He claimed he had an extra mouth to feed.

'Dad, Dad, come quickly! Mother's fighting a horrible twelve-foot monster with two heads and three arms!'
'Don't worry about it, son. I'm sure the monster can look after itself.'

FIRST MONSTER: I fancy eating the city of Hong Kong tonight. Care to join me?
SECOND MONSTER: *No thanks, I can't stand Chinese food.*

What do sea monsters have for dinner?
Fish and ships.

An enormous monster with eight arms and eleven legs walked into a tailor's shop. 'Quick!' shouted the tailor to his assistant. 'Hide the "Free Alterations" sign!'

What do you get if you cross King Kong with a giant frog?
A monster that climbs up the Empire State Building and catches aeroplanes with its tongue.

What's big and hairy and climbs up the Empire State Building in a dress?
Queen Kong.

Why did King Kong join the army?
To learn about gorilla warfare.

What's the best way to get King Kong to sit up and beg?
Wave a two-ton banana in front of his nose.

What do you call a witch's motor-bike?
A barooooom stick!

Monster graffiti: SAY IT WITH FLOWERS — GIVE HER A TRIFFID.

Where do ghost trains stop?
At a manifestation.

'Mummy, Mummy, what's a werewolf?'
'Shut up, and comb your face.'

Did you hear they now think the Loch Ness monster is a shark?
It's called Loch Jaws.

MR GHOST: You give me eerie ache.
MRS GHOST: *Sorry I spook!*

FIRST MONSTER: The bride of Frankenstein has a lovely face.
SECOND MONSTER: *If you can read between the lines.*

What do you call a monster moving through the leaves at midnight?
Russell.

Frankenstein's monster walks into a cafe and orders a cup of tea. 'That'll be £1,' said the waitress when she brought it to him. 'You know I was just thinking, we don't get many monsters in here . . .'

'I'm not surprised,' said Frankenstein's monster, 'at £1 a cup.'

How can you make a witch itch?
Take away her W.

Why does a monster lie on his back?
To trip low-flying aircraft.

'I bet I can get you to forget about the zombie.'
'What zombie?'
'See – you've forgotten already.'

Could you kill the Abominable Snowman just by throwing eggs at him?
Of course – he'd be eggs-terminated.

What do you get if you cross a zebra with an ape-man?
Tarzan stripes for ever!

What do you do if your pterodactyl is stolen?
Call the Flying Squad.

What is big and hairy and hangs on the line?
A drip-dry monster.

What's big and hairy and goes 'beep beep'?
A monster in a traffic jam.

What happened when King Kong swallowed Big Ben?
He found it time-consuming.

FIRST ZOMBIE: You look tired.
SECOND ZOMBIE: *Yes, I'm dead on my feet.*

Monster graffiti: VAMPIRES ARE A PAIN IN THE NECK!

How do monsters like their shepherd's pie?
Made with real shepherds.

What is a monster's favourite society?
The Consumers' Association.

How can you tell if a monster has a glass eye?
When it comes out in conversation.

Did you hear about the new Dracula Action Man?
You wind it up and it bites Sindy on the neck.

What did one skeleton prisoner say to the other skeleton prisoner?
If we had the guts, we'd get out of here.

Do you know the story about the body-snatchers?
Well, I won't tell you. You might get carried away.

MONSTER WOMAN: I have the face of a sixteen-year-old girl.
RUDE MONSTER BOY: *Well you'd better give it back then. You're getting it all wrinkled.*

FIRST HUMAN BOY: I can lift a monster with one hand.
SECOND HUMAN BOY: *Bet you can't!*
FIRST HUMAN BOY: Find me a monster with one hand and I'll prove it.

What do you get if you cross a witch with an ice cube?
A cold spell.

What are Dracula's favourite dogs?
Bloodhounds.

What is very tall and ugly and goes 'Eef if of muf?'
A backward giant.

JOHN MONSTER: Mum says we're having Aunty for Christmas dinner this year.
JANE MONSTER: *Well, she can't possibly be tougher than last year's turkey!*

What do you get if you cross a bird with a monstrous snarl?
A budgerigrrrrr!

FRED MONSTER: My sister must be twenty. I counted the rings under her eyes.
BERT MONSTER: *That's nothing. My sister's tongue is so long, she can lick an envelope after she's posted it.*

This little monster boy came home from school one day, crying his eyes out. 'What's the matter darling?' asked his mother.

'It's all the other children at school,' he sobbed. 'They keep teasing me and saying that I've got a big head.'

'Of course you haven't got a big head,' said Mrs Monster. 'Just ignore them. Now, will you do a little bit of shopping for me? I need a sack of potatoes, ten cartons of orange juice, a dozen loaves of bread, eight cabbages and a cauliflower.'

'All right, Mum,' said the little monster, 'but where's your shopping bag?'

'Oh, that's broken, I'm afraid,' said Mrs Monster, 'but it doesn't matter – just put the things in your cap.'

What's the difference between a musician and a corpse?
One composes, and the other decomposes.

What do you call a nervous sorceress?
A twitch.

What do you get if you cross a ghost with a packet of crisps?
Snacks that go crunch in the night.

What do you call a girl monster with one leg?
Eileen.

What do you get if you cross an owl with a monster?
A bird that's ugly but doesn't give a hoot.

What do you get if you cross a vampire with a mummy?
A flying bandage.

What do you get if you cross a vampire with a rose?
A flower that goes for your throat when you sniff it.

What happened to the wolf that fell into the washing machine?
It became a wash and werewolf.

How did the midget monster get into the police force?
He lied about his height.

Why did the monster eat candles?
For light refreshment.

FRED: Your monster was making a terrible noise last night.

BERT: *Yes – ever since he ate Madonna, he thinks he can sing.*

Mrs Monster has such an ugly baby she doesn't push the pram – she pulls it.

MONSTER TEACHER: If I had two people beside me, and you had two people beside you, what would we have?
MONSTER PUPIL: *Lunch!*

What do you call a twelve-foot long monster with a pointed head?
Lance.

Why is the monsters' football pitch wet?
Because the players keep dribbling on it.

What do you get if you cross the Abominable Snowman with Dracula?
Frostbite.

'Who's that at the door?
'The Invisible Man.'
'Tell him I can't see him.'

Knock, knock.
Who's there?
Lucretia.
Lucretia who?
Lucretia from the Black Lagoon.

What do you do if King Kong sits in front of you at the cinema?
Miss most of the film!

What did one witch say to the other witch when inviting her to supper?
'You'll just have to take pot luck!'

TEACHER: If you saw me standing by a monster, what fruit would it remind you of?
PUPIL: *A pear.*

If King Kong went to Hong Kong to play ping-pong and died, what would they put on his coffin?
A lid.

Where do vampires go for their holidays?
Bat-lins.

What do you get if you cross a prehistoric monster with a sleeping person?
A dinasnore.

Who did Dracula marry?
His ghoul-friend.

Where do ghosts send their laundry?
To the dry-screamers.

What is a skeleton's favourite pop group?
Boney M.

From the monster library:
The Vampire's Victim by E. Drew Blood
Chased By A Werewolf by Claude Bottom
The Omen by B. Warned
Foaming At The Mouth by Dee Monic
Creature From Mars by A. Lee-En
Horror Story by Denise R. Knockin
In The Monster's Jaws by Mandy Ceased
Frankenstein's Experiments by Tess Tube
Dracula by Pearce Nex
Poltergeists by Eve L. Spirit
Ghosts And Ghoulies by Sue Pernatural
Witch's Coven by De Ville Worshipper
Terrible Spells by B. Witcher

TEACHER: What followed the dinosaur?
PUPIL: *Its tail.*

What did the skeleton say to his friend?
'I've got a bone to pick with you.'

Why do some monsters eat raw meat?
Because they don't know how to cook.

What do you get if you cross an Egyptian mummy with a car mechanic?
Toot and Car Man.

What do you get if you cross a skeleton with a famous detective?
Sherlock Bones.

What did ET's mother say to him when he finally got home?
'Where on Earth have you been?'

What do you get if you cross an Egyptian mummy with a swot?
Someone who is wrapped up in his work.

'Doctor, doctor, I think I'm a witch!'
'You'd better lie down for a spell.'

What do you get if you cross a monster with Father Christmas?
Santa Claws.

What do you get if you cross an elephant with the abominable snowman?
A jumbo yeti!

What is the ghost's favourite Yuletide song?
'I'm Dreaming Of A Fright Christmas.'

How do monsters tell the future?
With horrorscopes.

What do you call the spot in the middle of a graveyard?
The dead centre.

How can you tell if a vampire has been at your tomato juice?
By the teeth marks on the lid.

TEACHER: What would you do if you saw a big monster?
PUPIL: *Hope it didn't see me!*

SISTER: What shall I do? My teacher says I've got to write an essay on a monster.
BROTHER: *Well first, you're going to need a very big ladder . . .*

What do you get if you leave bones out in the sun?
A skeletan!

Why did Dracula miss lunch?
Because he didn't fancy the stake.

MONSTER: Did you ever see anyone like me before?
HUMAN GIRL: *Yes, once. But I had to pay admission.*

What do monsters like eating most in restaurants?
The waiters!

What kind of book did Frankenstein's monster like to read?
One with a cemetery plot.

What is Dracula's favourite slogan?
Please Give Blood Generously.

Why did Doctor Frankenstein tiptoe past the medicine cabinet?
He didn't want to wake the sleeping pills.

Did you hear about the monster who fell into a barrel of beer?
He came to a bitter end.

Why is Dracula always happy to help young vampires?
Because he likes to see new blood in the business.

What does a zombie call its parents?
Mum and Dead.

When should you feed yeti's milk to a baby?
When it's a baby yeti.

Which musical instrument does a skeleton play?
A trom-bone.

What is a monster after it is one year old?
A two-year-old monster.

How can you get a set of teeth put in for free?
Smack a monster.

What do you get if you cross a monster with a boy scout?
A monster that scares old ladies across the street.

The two monsters went duck-hunting with their dogs, but without success. 'I know what it is, Zob,' said Grunge. 'I know what we're doing wrong.'

'What's that then, Grunge?'

'We're not throwing the dogs high enough.'

Tarzan climbed to the top of the highest mountain in the jungle. Suddenly, he was surrounded by every kind of hideous, fire-breathing, evil-smelling monster in creation – yetis, goblins, trolls, Martians, mekons, abominable snowmen, the lot. Do you know what he said? 'Boy, am I ever in the wrong joke . . .'

A very posh man was walking around an art gallery, when he stopped by one particular exhibit. 'I suppose this picture of a hideous monster is what you call modern art,' he said very pompously.

'No, sir,' replied the assistant, 'that's what we call a mirror.'

Did you hear about the very well-behaved little monster? When he was good his father would give him a penny and a pat on the head. By the time he was sixteen he had £25 in the bank and his head was totally flat . . .

What is the best way to see a monster?
On television.

FIRST MONSTER: I'm going to a party tonight.
SECOND MONSTER: *Oh, are you?*
FIRST MONSTER: Yes, I must go to the graveyard and dig out a few old friends.

How do you raise a baby monster that has been abandoned by its parents?
With a fork lift truck.

RUDE BOY: What's that horrible, ugly thing on your shoulders?
WOMAN: *I don't know, what is it?*
RUDE BOY: Your head!

What did the werewolf write on his Christmas cards?
Best vicious of the season.

What did the monster say when he saw the man sleeping?
'Ah, breakfast in bed!'

What do ghosts who have been in hospital love to do?
Talk about their apparitions.

Why don't monsters eat penguins?
Because they can't get the wrappers off.

What's the difference between an injured monster and bad weather?
One roars with pain, the other pours with rain.

Why do monsters scratch themselves?
Because they're the only ones who know where they itch.

What's the difference between a biscuit and a monster?
Ever tried dunking a monster?

Can a monster jump higher than a lamp post?
Yes – lamp posts can't jump.

BOY 1: I'm going to keep this monster under my bed.
BOY 2: *But what about the smell?*
BOY 1: He'll just have to get used to it.

What do you do if a monster feels sick?
Stand well back!

How do we know that S is a scary letter?
Because it makes cream scream.

In prehistoric times, what did they call shipping disasters at sea?
Tyrannosaurus wrecks.

Why does a barber never shave a monster with a forked tongue?
Because it's easier with a razor.

Who looks after sick gnomes?
The National Elf Service.

What is the biggest ghost in the world?
An elephantom.

What do you get if you cross a monster with a flea?
Lots of very worried dogs.

What do short-sighted ghosts wear?
Spook-tacles.

What kind of boats do vampires like?
Blood vessels.

Did you hear about the monster that has pedestrian eyes?
They look both ways before they cross.

What's a vampire's favourite tourist spot?
The Vampire State Building.

What walks through walls backwards, saying 'Boo' very quietly?
A nervous ghost.

Why does a witch ride on a broom?
A vacuum cleaner is too heavy.

What do you call a play that's acted by ghosts?
A phantomime.

What do ghosts eat for lunch?
Ghoul-ash.

What do ghosts eat for supper?
Spook-etti.

What is the difference between a very small witch and a deer that is running from a hunter?
One is a hunted stag, and the other is a stunted hag.

What do ghosts eat for breakfast?
Dreaded wheat.

FIRST MONSTER: We had burglars last night.
SECOND MONSTER: *Oh, did you?*
FIRST MONSTER: Well, it made a change from slime on toast.

What sort of soup do monsters like?
One with plenty of body in it.

MUMMY VAMPIRE: Jimmy, hurry up and drink your soup before it clots.

MICKEY MONSTER: Look Mum, I've brought a friend home for lunch.
MOTHER MONSTER: *Good! Well, shove him in the oven.*

MONSTER TO DAUGHTER: You know, you really should be looking for an edible young bachelor.

What did the mother ghost say to the baby ghost?
'Spook when you're spoken to.'

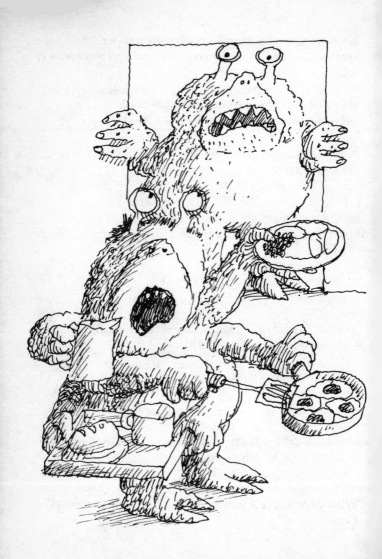

MR MONSTER: Oi, hurry up with my supper!
MRS MONSTER: *Oh, do be quiet – I've only got three pairs of hands.*

Why couldn't the skeleton go to the ball?
Because he had no body to go with.

Where do ghosts stay when they go on holiday?
At a ghost-house.

What do you get if you cross a biscuit with a monster?
Crumbs.

What do you get if you cross a monster with a pig?
Large pork chops.

What do you get if you cross a monster with peanut butter?
A monster that sticks to the roof of your mouth.

What do you call a monster that has written a book?
An author.

What do you call a monster in a jumbo jet?
A passenger.

What's green, seven feet tall, and mopes in the corner?
The Incredible Sulk.

What's green and wrinkled?
The Incredible Sulk's granny.

What do you get if you cross a monster with a kangaroo?
Big holes across Australia.

What has 22 legs, 11 heads, 2 wings and goes crunch?
A football team eating crisps.

What is big, slimy and ugly – and very blue?
A monster holding its breath.

What do you get if you cross a monster with a pigeon?
Lots of very worried pedestrians.

What do you get if you cross a monster with a skunk?
A big, ugly smell!

If you saw 9 monsters outside Woolworth's with blue socks and one monster outside Boots with red socks, what would that prove?
That 9 out of 10 monsters wear blue socks.

A man was walking behind a hearse with a big monster on a lead. Behind them stretched a long line of mourners.
  'What happened?' asked a passer-by.
  'The monster bit my wife, and she died of fright.'
  'Can I borrow it?' the passer-by asked.
  The man pointed behind him. 'Get in the queue,' he said.

SLIMY MONSTER: What would I have to give you to get a little kiss?
BEAUTIFUL GIRL: *Chloroform.*

MRS MONSTER TO MR MONSTER: Try to be nice to my mother when she visits us this weekend, dear. Fall down when she hits you.

RUDE BOY TO WOMAN MONSTER: Is that your real face or are you wearing a gas-mask?
WOMAN MONSTER: *I didn't come here to be insulted.*
RUDE BOY: Oh, where do you usually go?

86

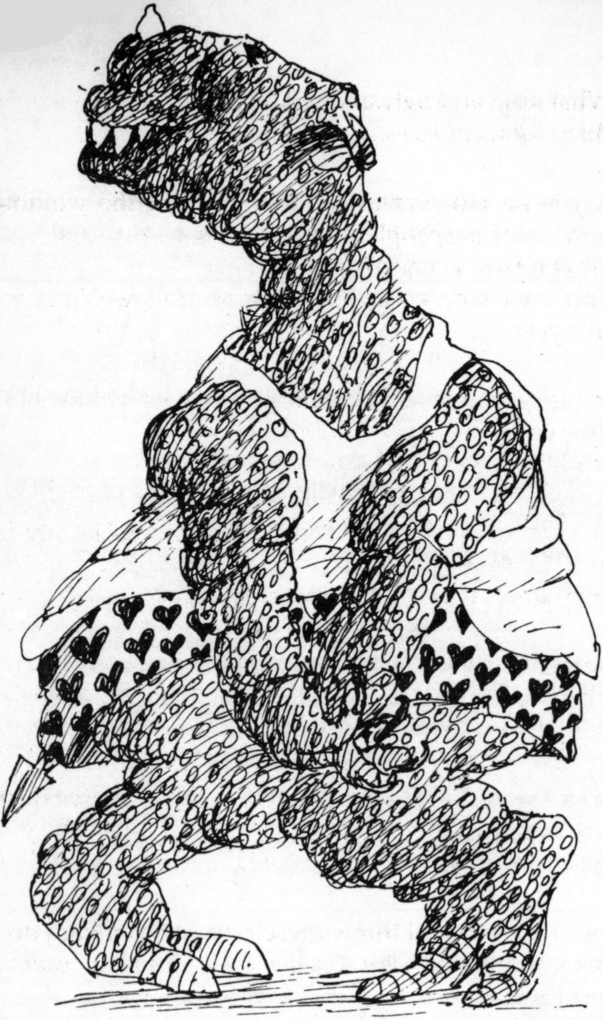

What's big and ugly and red all over?
An embarrassed monster.

BROTHER MONSTER: Don't look out of the window –
you'll confuse people.
SISTER MONSTER: *What do you mean?*
BROTHER MONSTER: They'll think Hallowe'en is early
this year.

JULIET MONSTER: You remind me of my favourite boxer.
ROMEO MONSTER: *Barry McGuigan?*
JULIET MONSTER: No, his name is Fido.

MILLIE MONSTER: Do you think I should let my hair
grow?
MAX MONSTER: *Yes – right over your face.*

BOY MONSTER: You remind me of the ocean.
GIRL MONSTER: *Oh, romantic, wild, untamed and restless?*
BOY MONSTER: No, you make me sick.

MARY MONSTER: I wish I had a pound for every boy that
has asked me to marry him.
MARTIN MONSTER: *What would you buy – a bag of crisps?*

FRED MONSTER: I throw myself into everything I do.
DICK MONSTER: *Then why don't you go and dig yourself a
nice big hole?*

How do dinosaurs pass exams?
With extinction!

Did you hear about the cannibal who went on a self-catering holiday and ate himself?

How do you keep an ugly monster in suspense?
I'll tell you tomorrow . . .

What do you call a twenty foot monster with a machine gun?
Sir!

How do ghosts travel?
On fright trains.

GIRL MONSTER TO HER FRIEND: I think my brother was
born upside down.
FRIEND: *Oh, why's that?*
GIRL MONSTER: His nose runs, and his feet smell.

What happened to the monster who ran away with the circus?
The police made him bring it back.

Why does a vampire clean his teeth three times a day?
To prevent bat breath.

What eats its victims two by two?
Noah's shark.

Who is in charge of a haunted police station?
The in-spectre.

How do you make a monster fly?
Start with a ten-foot zip . . .

What is a ghost's favourite book?
Ghoul-liver's Travels.

How do English ghosts go abroad?
By British Scareways.

What monster makes funny noises in its throat?
A gargoyle.

What did the ghost call his mother and father?
His transparents.

How can you tell if a ghost is about to faint?
It goes as white as a sheet.

FIRST BOY: I met a ghost last night.
SECOND BOY: *What did it say?*
FIRST BOY: I don't know – I can't speak dead languages.

If you tipped a can of food over a ghoul, what would you get?
Beans on ghost.

What do you call a monster who likes sewing?
Fred.

What do you call a monster with a car on his head?
Jack.

What do you call a girl monster who's loaded with money?
Kitty.

What do you call a girl monster who takes your coat?
Peg.

What do you call a monster who spends a lot of time in church?
Neal.

What do you get if you cross a monster with a watchdog?
Very nervous postmen!

How do you get a monster into a matchbox?
Take all the matches out first.

What time is it when a monster puts his left foot on your right foot?
Time to call an ambulance.

Why do some monsters have big ears?
Noddy wouldn't pay the ransom.

How can you tell if there's a monster in your fridge?
You can't shut the door.

How can you tell if a monster has been in your fridge?
By the footprints in the butter.

How can you tell if there's a monster under your bed?
When your face is nearly touching the ceiling.

Monster graffiti: GET THE MONSTER BEFORE IT GETS
AAARRGGH!

What do you get if you cross a hairdresser with a were-wolf?
A monster with an all-over perm.

A man's car broke down on a cold and wind-swept night, near an eerie looking castle in Transylvania. The wizened old butler invited him to stay the night, and showed him to his room. It was dark and dirty, and the man was scared.

'I hope you'll be comfortable,' said the butler. 'But if you need anything during the night, just scream . . .'

'Doctor, doctor, you must help me'
'What's the problem?'
'Every night, I dream there are terrible green and yellow slimy monsters under my bed. What on earth can I do?'
'Saw the legs off your bed.'

What's a vampire's worst enemy?
Fang decay.

'Doctor, doctor, you've got to help me – I keep dreaming of bats, creepy-crawlies, demons, ghosts, monsters, vampires, werewolves and yetis . . .'
'How very interesting! Do you always dream in alphabetical order?'

What was the inscription on the tomb of Frankenstein's monster?
HERE LIES FRANKENSTEIN'S MONSTER. MAY HE REST IN PIECES.

What's Dracula's favourite coffee?
De-coffin-ated.

What did the monster say to his psychiatrist?
'I feel abominable.'

Sign at a witches' demo: WE DEMAND SWEEPING
REFORMS!

Why doesn't Dracula have any friends?
Because he's such a pain in the neck.

What do you call a wicked old woman who lives by the sea?
A sand-witch.

What happens when monsters hold beauty contests?
Nobody wins.

Why do werewolves do well at school?
Because every time they're asked a question, they come up with a snappy answer.

What do you get if you cross a Rolls-Royce with a vampire?
A monster that attacks expensive cars and sucks out their petrol tanks.

Why are vampire families close?
Because blood is thicker than water.

MONSTER MOTHER: How many times have I told you not to eat with your fingers? Use the spade like everyone else.

Where does the bride of Frankenstein have her hair done?
At the ugly parlour.

Why is the graveyard such a noisy place?
Because of all the coffin.

What does a monster do when he loses a hand?
He goes to a second-hand shop.

What do you get if you cross a Scottish monster with a hamburger?
A Big Mac.

What kind of horse would a headless horseman ride?
A nightmare.

What do you call a monster who has fallen into the sea and can't swim?
Bob.

What do you call a monster with no legs?
It doesn't matter what you call him, he still won't come.

How do you make a monster float?
Take two scoops of ice-cream, a glass of Coke and add one monster . . .

Why did the dinosaur cross the road?
Because there weren't any chickens in those days.

What do you call a dinosaur who's been dead and buried
for a million years?
Pete.

What do you call a drunken ghost?
A methylated spirit.

Did you hear about the two blood cells?
They loved in vein.

What is a monster's favourite game?
Swallow the leader.

What do ghosts wear in the rain?
Boo-ts and ghoul-oshes.

DRACULA: We're going on holiday tomorrow.
DRACULA'S WIFE: *Remind me to cancel our daily pint of
blood.*

Why do ghosts like tall buildings?
Because they have lots of scarecases.

What does a vegetarian monster eat?
Swedes.

Where do ghosts go swimming?
In the Dead Sea.

FIRST GHOST: I don't seem to frighten people any more.
SECOND GHOST: *I know. We might as well be dead, for all they care.*

FIRST GHOST: I find haunting castles really boring these days.
SECOND GHOST: *I know what you mean. I just don't seem able to put any life into it.*

FIRST MONSTER: I don't think much of your wife.
SECOND MONSTER: *Never mind – eat the vegetables instead.*

JOHNNY: Dad, what has a purple body with yellow spots, eight hairy legs and big slimy eyes on stalks?
DAD: *I don't know. Why?*
JOHNNY: Because one's just crawled up your trouser leg.

The ghoul stood on the bridge one night,
Its lips were all a-quiver;
It gave a cough,
Its leg fell off
And floated down the river.

Which monster has no luck?
The luckless monster.

What did the cannibal say to the famous missionary?
'Doctor Livingstone, I consume?'

What do you call a monster with a tree on his head?
Edward.

What do you call a monster with three trees on his head?
Edward Woodward.

MONSTER: How much do you charge for dinner here?
WAITER: *£20 a head, sir.*
MONSTER: And how much for a couple of legs, as well?

WAITER ON THE *QE2:* Would you like the menu, sir?
MONSTER: *No thanks, just bring me the passenger list.*

What do you find in a haunted cellar?
Whines and spirits.

What position does a ghost play in a football team?
Ghoulie.

Why are cemeteries so popular?
Who knows, but people are dying to get into them!

Why did the monster go into hospital?
To have his ghoul-stones removed.

What do you call a stupid monster?
A dummy mummy.

How do monsters like their eggs?
Terror-fried.

HOW TO CATCH A BIG MONSTER
First, get a telescope, a matchbox, a pair of tweezers,
and a very long, boring book. Then choose a hot day

and go to any place where you know big monsters live.

Sit down with the telescope, matchbox and tweezers next to you, and start to read the long, boring book. After a while you'll fall asleep, because the book is so dull and the day is so hot.

Soon a big monster is bound to see you and come over to investigate. Looking over your shoulder, he will start to read the long, boring book and he, too, will fall asleep from boredom and the heat.

As soon as he does, you must wake up, pick up the telescope, and look at the big sleeping monster through the wrong end. Then, using your tweezers, pick him up carefully, put him in the matchbox, and lo and behold – you have caught a big monster!

Two monsters walked along the beach at Brighton. One said to the other, *'Not much of a crowd for a bank holiday, is there?'*

BIOLOGY TEACHER: What is a blood count?
PUPIL: *Dracula*.

There once was a monster called Fred,
Who used to eat garlic in bed;
His mother said, 'Son,
That's not really done,
Why don't you eat people instead?'

'The police are looking for a monster with one eye called Cyclops.'
'What's his other eye called?'

What do you get if you cross Dracula with Sir Lancelot?
A bite in shining armour.

Who was the first prehistoric novelist?
Charlotte Brontesaurus.

What weighed 20 stone and terrorized Paris?
The Fat-Tum of the Opera.

What did the doctor say to the Invisible Man's wife?
'I can't see anything wrong with your husband.'